)))))))

Raves for Perception

"One thing I learned during my years as CEO is that perception matters. And in these times when public confidence and trust have been shaken, I've learned the hard way that perception matters more than ever."

Jack Welch, former CEO and Chairman
General Electric, Wall Street Journal, 9/16/02

"Bush has to quickly improve conditions in Iraq while limiting the perception that the U.S. is an occupying power."

Business Week Magazine, 4/2/03

"It took us a long time to get into the rankings because of the perception that we were a young team that wasn't going to be ready."

Jim Boeheim, Syracuse basketball coach
on CBS after winning the Final Four, 4/7/03

"Perception, perception, perception...this will go down badly."

Dennis Kozlowski
Former CEO of Worldcom
New Yorker magazine, 2/17/03

(On Nike's failure to dominate golf equipment)
"The company has not been able to persuade golfers, well schooled by Callaway, to look at a Big Bertha without feeling an extra ten yards coming."
Douglas B. Holt, Ass't Professor
Harvard Business School
New Yorker letter-to-the editor, 7/15/02

"People only see what they are prepared to see."
Ralph Waldo Emerson, American author

"Money itself isn't lost or made, it's simply transferred from one perception to another."
Oliver Stone, American filmmaker

"I think you will agree that perception is more important than reality."
Mark Haynes, Host of CNBC's Squawk Box,
discussing the SARS virus and the economy, 4/28/03

"An optimist sees an opportunity in every calamity. A pessimist sees a calamity in every opportunity."
Sir Winston Churchill, British statesman

"You never really understand a person until you consider things from his point of view...until you climb inside of his skin and walk around in it."
To Kill a Mockingbird

"The popularity of disaster movies...expresses a collective perception of a world threatened by irresistible and unforeseen forces which nevertheless are thwarted at the last moment."
David Mamet, American playwright

"The intention of psychoanalysis is to strengthen the ego, to make it more independent of the superego, to widen its field of perception..."
Sigmund Freud, Austrian psychiatrist

"The solution to stress management lies in how we perceive the stresses in our lives."
Doc Childre and Howard Martin
The HeartMath Solution

"Everyone has beauty, but not everyone sees it."
Confucious, Chinese philosopher

*THIS BOOK IS
DEDICATED
TO MY MOTHER,*

*THE VOICE OF
THE EAGLE*

Published by BullsEye, LLC

For information about books in the PERCEPTION RULES! series, BullsEye Branding training and consulting program and merchandise, see pages 116-121.

Visit our website at www.perceptionrules.net

First printing, September 2003

ISBN 0-9744885-0-X

LCCN 2003096170

Printed in the United States of America

Graphic Design by Lyndsay W Beauchamp
Creative Director: V Harris

Table of Contents

Chapter One   *The Early Years*
Chapter Two   *Perception **is** Reality*
Chapter Three   *No Surprises*
Chapter Four   *A Painful Lesson*
Chapter Five   *Another World*
Chapter Six   *Ring of Fire*
Chapter Seven   *Out To Pasture*
Chapter Eight   *An Eagle Eye*
Chapter Nine   *Powerful Influences*
Chapter Ten   *The Rule of Three*
Chapter Eleven   *Know Yourself*
Chapter Twelve   *Don't Lose Control*
Chapter Thirteen   *Branding Yourself*
Chapter Fourteen   *The PvP Principle*™
Chapter Fifteen   *Branding Someone You Know*
Chapter Sixteen   *Practice Makes Perfect*
Chapter Seventeen *Picture This!*

The 7 Rules of Perception™

Exercise Assessments

Questions to Ask Yourself

Services

))))))

Preface

My fascination with the power of perception goes back to my youth. Being tall for my age, I was keenly aware how my being "different" impacted the way I was perceived. Then, when my mother was widowed at age 36, I watched her cope with being a woman alone, how this impacted how she perceived herself, as well as how she was perceived by the "couples world;" then the business world as she developed her career. These and other memories heightened my sensitivity to the powerful impact that perception has on personal success.

Later, as the founder of a successful marketing communications company, I developed and refined my concepts about perception with my clients – brand leaders such as Kodak, Corning, and Chase Manhattan, as well as new business start-ups, institutions, even politicians.

PERCEPTION RULES! is based not on theory, therefore, but on lots of practical experience. While everyone knows the cliché, "Perception is Reality," just what does this mean? How does it work? And how can you gain control of perception for your own benefit?

The Story of Brandin, the Misunderstood Bull, is designed to fill this void...to help you understand how your own "Personal Brand" or image is controlled by how you perceive yourself, and how *others* perceive you. Through Brandin's transformation, you will learn how perception impacts your ability to succeed in life: to communicate effectively; build self-confidence; get a job, and keep it; manage stress; and navigate change.

PERCEPTION RULES! It impacts the strength of every brand – be it a person, a product, a business, an institution, or an organization. The same rules apply.

Fact is: perception has a profound influence on critical business functions from management effectiveness and sales success, to office politics, customer satisfaction, and diversity issues. It plays a critical role in hiring and firing, job satisfaction, and relationships of every kind.

Perception, in sum, plays a key role in your ability to succeed in every part of life – at home, in your community, and at the office. It would please me no end if you find inspiration from reading my book to communicate to the world the best you that you can possibly be!

V Harris
September, 2003

V HARRIS

꒞ ꒞ ꒞

Chapter One
The Early Years

One starry, summer night at the Double M Ranch deep in the heart of Texas, a most commonly cow named Molly gave birth to a baby bull. And lickety split, the baby bull stood up on his wobbly legs and let out an amazing snort of glee!

"Did you see that?" exclaimed his owner, Morton Murphy. "At long last, I've got me a strong, handsome champion! We're gonna win every blue ribbon at every breedin' show from here to San Antonio. This is no ordinary bull, no sireee, this is a whole new brand of bull!"

And that's how Brandin got his name.

As the summer days moved through August into September, Brandin grew bigger and stronger.

Life was good at the Morton Murphy Double M Ranch. Brandin loved running around the huge pastures chasing bees hiding in alfalfa flowers, and watching his mother, Molly, and his sisters chewing their cuds. He felt secure and much loved.

Then one day, some tourists passing by the ranch stopped their car, and out spilled a family who walked right up to the fence, cameras in hand, to take pictures of the animals in the pasture.

Brandin was so excited to see new faces and to have his picture taken that he ran fast as he could straight towards the fence. Whereupon the most astonishing thing happened. The tourists dropped their cameras and ran fast as they could back to their car in utter fright!

"Now whatever made them do that?" Brandin wondered. "I just wanted to say hi."

As the car tore off, one of the terrorized tourists hung out the window and screamed, "You shouldn't let mean, scary, dangerous bulls like that frighten people. It's downright criminal!"

))))))

Chapter Two
Perception Is Reality

Brandin did not sleep a wink as he tried to make sense out of what had happened. Why were those people afraid of him? What did they see in him that he didn't understand?

Big, bull-sized tears welled up in his eyes and dribbled down his face. Brandin had never felt lonely before, but that night he felt very alone, very confused, and very misunderstood.

His mother, Molly, did her best to try and comfort him. "You've got to understand what being a bull is all about, Brandin, and why people think that bulls are mean, scary, and dangerous brutes."

"But, that's not me," Brandin said sadly. "I don't want to hurt anyone."

"I know, my son. I see you as the friendliest, gentlest, kindest bull that ever lived. But, others see horns sprouting from your head, and those horns are lethal weapons capable of killing. That's why you're perceived as mean, scary and dangerous – even though that's not at all the real you."

Brandin was completely and totally confused. He had no idea what being a bull was about. He couldn't see his horns. He had never seen his Father. In fact, he had never seen any other bulls in his short life at the ranch. But obviously, how he saw himself was not the way he was seen by others.

The more Brandin thought about his dilemma, the more depressed he became. He stopped running around the pasture and sat for hours in his pen, his head drooped in total dejection.

⋙ ⋙ ⋙

Chapter Three
No Surprises

"What are we going to do with this bull of ours?" Morton Murphy shouted to his wife at the dinner table.

"What the devil is wrong with him? I've never seen a bull cry – have you? That's the saddest, stubbornest, most worthless bull I've ever seen! And here I thought we had ourselves a strong, handsome champion!"

"I'll go talk to him," murmured Muriel Murphy, trying to soften her husband's growing anger. So out she went to the bull pen, and kneeled down so that her face was close to Brandin's.

"Whatever is wrong with you?" she whispered in his ear. "You've got to get yourself out of this slump that you're in, Brandin. Please try and act like a bull. For heaven's sake don't let this mean, scary, dangerous image of the tourist get you down. Be fearless, strong and brave, the way bulls are supposed to behave, don't you know?"

"No, I don't know," Brandin blurted out. "And I don't want to be a bull anymore. I wish I was a gentle, happy, contented cow like my mother and my sisters. Nobody's scared of cows."

"Of course not," Muriel Murphy replied. "I never met a cow that wasn't gentle, happy and contented. In fact, the reason why I love cows is because there are no surprises.

"The way I see a cow is exactly the way it is in reality, Muriel continued. "A cow is one thing I know I can trust. Like John Wayne. He never changed from one movie to another. John Wayne is John Wayne. Same with Elvis. And Dolly Parton. And Harry Truman.

I like it when what I see is what I get."

Muriel Murphy was silent for a moment, then she added, "What I don't care for are actors who keep changing their image. It makes me nervous."

Brandin listened in silence. He understood what she was saying, but he didn't know how he could make people see him as fearless, strong and brave instead of mean, scary and dangerous.

꒐ ꒐ ꒐

Chapter Four
A Painful Lesson

When Muriel went back and reported to her husband that Brandin still didn't seem to get it, Morton went into a rage. "I'm gonna show that damn bull what b.s. is all about!" And out the door he flew – whip in hand – and stormed straight to the bull pen.

"Get up, you weak, pathetic, disgrace of a bull!" And when Brandin didn't move, Morton flicked his wrist, sending the whip straight towards Brandin's hind quarters.

The sting shocked Brandin, and he lurched to his feet, eyes fixed on Morton Murphy with amazement.

Then a second sting, even stronger than the first, hit his side. At that, with nostrils flaring, Brandin leapt towards Morton Murphy and backed him right into the corner of the pen.

Morton stood frozen, waiting for Brandin to attack. But he simply stood there, staring at his owner, a very sad look crossing his eyes – a look that Morton Murphy had never before seen in a bull.

In a state of total perplexion, Morton scrambled quickly under the fence, ran home, picked up the phone and – in a voice suddenly and suspiciously soft and soothing – called the nearest bull agent.

"I've got a big, powerful champion here at my ranch. Come tomorrow and he's yours!"

))) •)) •))

Chapter Five
Another World

A fly buzzing about Brandin's head rose him from his recurring nightmare of his youth at the Double M Ranch, and that first moment when he realized that he was not seen by others as he saw himself.

Brandin drifted off to sleep and his dream continued. He saw himself leaving the Double M Ranch, being loaded onto a plane, and ending up hours later in a strange country where the people spoke a language that he had never heard before.

"Toro guapo y fuerte! – whatever does that mean?" Brandin thought to himself.

He now shared a pasture on the outskirts of a medieval town with five other 1,500 pound bulls. One had a broken horn and was named Lunatic! "If this is what a bull looks like, I can understand why those tourists ran away from me," Brandin muttered under his breath .

A soft rain fell, and the air was heavy with the smell of barbecued pig. Rowdy revelers drinking cheap champagne danced the night away with wild abandon.

Early the next morning, Brandin and the other bulls were herded into the Plaza of the nearby town. At precisely 8:00 a.m. a loud rocket was launched setting the startled bulls into a frantic stampede.

Confused by the noise, Brandin found himself running full speed around a sharp curve into a narrow street paved with slick, slippery cobblestones. People hung out of windows cheering wildly as a bawdy group of fool-hardy men (and several women) with red scarves around their necks, and red sashes around their waists, scurried into doorways to avoid being gored or trampled by the hard charging bulls.

When the frightening event ended, Brandin was grateful to return to his pen and try to sort out the day's chaotic events. His fellow bulls were pawing, snorting, and standing tall to show off their horns, but Brandin paid no attention.

He just wanted to be left alone.

The sight of medics scurrying around to care for those injured in the annual rite called the "Running of the Bulls" horrified him.

Brandin now understood why he was perceived as mean, scary and dangerous. This saddened him because he knew this was not his true self.

Even worse, he had no idea what he could do about it.

)))

Chapter Six
Ring of Fire

As Brandin's dream continued, he saw himself being sent to a huge building and locked in a pen in its dank and dark basement.

He was alone for nearly a week listening to water dripping down the stone walls, until one Saturday, a man came and opened the door of his pen. Ahead, Brandin saw the light at the end of a long, dark tunnel.

Tentatively, he stepped towards the light, slowly picking up speed at the thought that he might, in fact, be able to run away and be free!

As he approached the end of the tunnel, a door suddenly snapped open, and Brandin charged ahead only to find himself in a huge arena that erupted into the loudest cheering that he ever heard.

Stunned, he stopped dead in his tracks, confused at the sight of so many people in the stands.

"Whatever are all these people doing here?" Brandin wondered.

And then, a man wearing a three cornered, black hat and a tight jacket and pants embroidered with gold threads scrambled over a wall, and stood very still and erect, holding a red cape in his right hand.

The sight of the red cape totally mesmerized Brandin. The sound of the cheering dimmed in his brain and in slow motion, he moved closer and closer towards the cape that the man held in front of his body.

Instinctively, Brandin lowered his head and charged, but just as he reached the cape, the man took a step sideways to avoid being gored by Brandin's horns.

In unison the crowd roared, "Olé!"

Over a period of two, three, then four hours, this same series of movements were repeated again and again. Brandin charged the red cape and once again the crowd shouted "Ole!"

And this determination in Brandin was what led to the longest bull fight in history. The man called the matador could not wear Brandin down no matter how hard he tried. Weary as he was of playing the game a calm, resolute voice in Brandin kept saying, "Don't quit, don't give up."

The afternoon wore on into early evening and shadows began to appear in the sweltering hot, dusty arena. As the moon began to rise in the sky, the matador suddenly reeled around and fainted onto the dry, dirt floor of the arena.

The crowd grew silent as they watched the strong, determined bull standing all alone in the ring doing nothing to hurt the matador.

They knew they were seeing a brave bull with a big heart.

꒰꒱ ꒰꒱ ꒰꒱

Chapter Seven
Out To Pasture

Brandin was roused from his dream by the scent of a creature hiding in a nearby bush. As he lifted his head, Brandin's eyes scanned the majestic mountains rising above the floor of the valley that he had grown to love.

As fate would have it, an American in the stands at the bull fight, so moved by what he had witnessed, purchased Brandin on the spot, and shipped him to his ranch in the north country of Wyoming.

Brandin had, literally, been put out to pasture because of his strong breeding lines. His reverie was abruptly disrupted when an animal that looked like a small wolf with big, pointed ears, and eerie, yellow eyes scampered out of the bush.

"I've been hunting all night, and can't find a darn thing to eat. Not a chicken or a rabbit. Not even a scrawny rodent. How can you stand it here? By the way, my name's Kyle Otey. I'd say, 'glad to meet you,' but I'm in no mood for pleasantries right now."

Brandin immediately felt sorry for the cocky creature who had plopped down by a rock in utter exhaustion. They struck up a conversation and Brandin soon found himself sharing the travails of his life, and his sadness at not being perceived as he truly was.

"Now, wait just a minute!" Kyle Otey protested. "Talk about bad perception! How'd ya like to be compared with wolves: the mean, nasty villains in fairy tales? Truth be told, I spend most of my time all alone, covering thousands of square miles trying to find myself a good, square meal.

"I'm talkin' survival, not sport, if you get the drift. And what do people think of me? Not as a clever, resourceful survivor who mates for life, and rarely goes after livestock, but as some sly, sneaky, shifty varmint that you shoot on sight. Tell me if that's fair?

"And speaking of bad raps, Kyle Otey continued, "Look what the movie Jaws did to sharks. Created mass hysteria! Just say the word, 'shark,' and you think fear, danger, and death. But, in reality, your chances of being struck by lightening are greater than being attacked by a shark. Poor things actually have to be protected from human beings who are fishing them to death for shark fin soup!"

Kyle Otey paused for a moment, thinking back to Brandin's life story. "So am I hearing you correctly? Your big problem is: you don't think you deserve to be perceived as a big, mean, scary bull?

"Well get over it. Give the people out there what they want, I say! In corporate America, the big cheeses are forever playing roles, trying to live up to preconceived notions of power and success.

"Just look at yourself, Brandin, for cripes sake! You really ARE big, strong, and powerful. So what if you're not mean, scary, and dangerous. Haven't you ever heard of the power of intimidation? Play to the crowd, I say! In nature, creatures are forever pretending to be one thing while in reality being quite another. It's called camouflage.

"Ever seen a Venus Fly Trap?"

Flush with pleasure over the brilliance of his insight, the coyote resumed his resting position against the rock, when all of a sudden, his yellow eyes widened bigger than a tennis ball. "Lordy, get me out of here!" he yelped.

⫘ ⫘ ⫘

Chapter Eight
An Eagle Eye

Before Brandin and Kyle Otey knew what was happening, a huge bird with long, wide wings swooped down out of the clear, blue sky.

"Oh, stop crouching in terror!" the Eagle admonished the cowering coyote. "First off, I just caught myself a tasty trout, and I can't stand the flavor of coyote meat. I also can't stand the advice that I heard you giving this bull who seems like a nice enough fellow, but a bit confused.

"Remember, we eagles can see the forest through the trees. You didn't know it, but I was resting on a cliff listening to your entire conversation, and Brandin – I'm here to tell you – this coyote is a shameless, sneaky, not to be trusted advisor.

"Oh, I know all about perception versus reality. We eagles may look strong and powerful, but my skeleton is hollow and filled with air. My bones actually weigh less than my 7,000 feathers, but I don't let that affect my image. I'm a veritable raptor; a flying hunting machine with a beak as sharp as a knife, and lethal claws that act like a fork."

"Well that's all well and good," Kyle Otey smirked, "but just like me, you eagles almost became extinct!"

"Quite true," the Eagle replied. "I could play the victim, and complain about the carelessness of hunters, and the abuse of the environment that almost wiped out my species. But I prefer to identify with my strength and my power."

With wings spread wide, the Eagle proclaimed: "I see my image on the standards of Imperial Rome and the Czars of Russia.

"I see religions all over the world depicting me as the sun or a god.

"And let's not forget that the eagle is the national symbol of America: the strongest, most powerful nation on earth.

"My perception IS my reality. And I'm not about to let anyone or anything change it!"

"But, what if we don't have your strength and self-confidence?" Brandin asked.

"Speak for yourself!" Kyle Otey declared. "I've got a darn healthy sense of self-esteem, and where does it get me? I can see myself as God's gift to coyotes 'til my eyes turn blue, but that doesn't stop others from perceiving me as a sly, sneaky, shifty varmint. Drives me crazy!"

"Exactly, the Eagle agreed. Any other person's perception may be quite at odds with yours – but that's their reality. Take a couple shopping for a car.

"The husband may perceive the salesman as knowledgeable, savvy, and persuasive while his wife sees the same salesperson as sexist, pushy, and phony. But, try to tell the salesperson that. It's difficult to understand how two people can see you so completely differently.

"Seems we're all blessed with self-awareness.

"The fact is, Perception Rules every imaginable part of our private and public lives – at home and at the office: getting a job or a promotion; making a date or getting a mate; buying or selling a house; coping with death and divorce; coming to grips with aging – the list is endless."

And with that, the Eagle flew off promising to return the next day with more insight about The 7 Rules of Perception.

Rule 1:
Perception *Is* Reality

**How you perceive yourself,
(or any other person)
is *your* reality.**

**How any *other* person
perceives you
(whether fair or not)
is *his* or *her* reality.**

Chapter Nine
Powerful Influences

The next morning, the Eagle made the following observation: "Perception doesn't just happen in a vacuum. There are many powerful influences that impact how our perceptions are formed."

"You're telling me!" Kyle Otey remarked. We coyotes are victims of all kinds of myth and superstition. Maybe it's due to my yellow eyes, but you wouldn't believe some of the stories I hear."

"And what about you, Brandin? What influences a person's perception about bulls?"

"I guess our horns look dangerous to the average person."

"Exactly," the Eagle replied. "Before you have said or done anything, a person may have already formed a preconceived perception about what a bull is like. I have always liked the way Ralph Waldo Emerson put it: 'People only see what they are prepared to see.'

"How others perceive you, is based NOT on what you say, or thought you said. It's what *others* hear, what they *think* you meant, what they *want* to believe.

"Stereotypes work this way. An opinion, attitude, or judgment of a person, a race, an issue, or an event is repeated over and over again and again without variation until every member of a group shares the same mental image. Stereotypes are oversimplified opinions. So is profiling.

"I say the following with a profound sense of sadness, Brandin, for you and Kyle Otey are not alone in being singled out unfairly. When the tourist screamed that you were mean, scary, and dangerous, you were a victim of profiling. And profiling of any kind is not fair, but it happens all the time. It's a very negative form of Personal Branding!"

"You've got that right!" Kyle Otey blurted out. "Ask anyone who is African, Arab, Asian, Hispanic, or Native American, elderly, disabled, homosexual, or just looks like a coyote. How do ya think I got my identity crisis? Profiling, prejudice, discrimination, exclusion – whatever you call it, there's no respect for the individual."

"Exactly," the Eagle agreed. "Each of us deserves to be treated with dignity and respect."

After a period of silence – because the impact of what the Eagle, Brandin and Kyle Otey were discussing had really hit home – the Eagle suggested that they make a list of the factors that influence how our perceptions are formed.

Rule 2:
Powerful Influences

**Many factors influence
how you form your perceptions
about yourself and others,
and how others
form their perceptions
about you.**

- *The five senses (from the Latin, senses: the faculty of perceiving) – sight, hearing, smell, touch, and taste.*

- *Race
  nationality
  ethnic background*

- *Gender*

- *Age*

- *Personality*

- *Language*

- *Type of work*

- *Income*

- *Place of residence*

- *Marital state and number of children*

- *Sexual orientation*

- *Health – physical and psychological*

- *Emotional make-up, attitude, mood, sensitivities, anxieties, fears, worries, and concerns*

- *Height, weight, shape*

- *Personal appearance – clothing, hair, make-up, jewelry, etc.*

- *Body language, posture, mannerisms*

- *Verbal clues such as tone of voice*

- *Religion – or lack of it*

- *Upbringing*

- *Memories – good and bad*

- *Family views, biases and influences*

- *Level of intelligence*

- *Creativity and imagination*

- *Education – where it took place,
  who did the educating, and for how long*

- *Reputation*

- *Myth, superstition*

- *The media:
  books, newspapers, magazines
  radio, television, films*

- *Views of business, religious,
  political, and community leaders*

- *What friends and those you admire
  say, think, eat, drink, drive, and wear*

- *Clubs, organizations, unions,
  and other affiliations*

∂⟫ ∂⟫ ∂⟫

Chapter Ten
The Rule of Three

Reviewing the many factors that influence perception was so exhausting that the Eagle decided to give Brandin and Kyle Otey a day off before meeting again. It was a bright, sunny morning when the Eagle returned, wings aglow with a golden light.

"Remember when we last three met, I told you how I identify with my strength and my power, and that my perception is my reality? The point is: how do you expect to be perceived positively by others if you don't perceive yourself in a positive manner?

"With this in mind, I'd like both of you to consider how you can gain control of perception.

And I'll give you a big hint: it begins within each of us – having a positive self-image, and a healthy amount of self-esteem. I'll talk more about this later. But first tell me this Brandin, when was the first time you felt that others did not perceive you as you perceive yourself?"

Brandin recounted his early days at the Double M Ranch. How shocked he was when the tourists ran away. How sad he was to hear himself described as mean, scary, and dangerous. And how powerless he felt in the face of it."

"O.K.," the Eagle said, "it's not nice to be seen as mean, scary, and dangerous, but what the tourist yelled at you was your first clue, Brandin. The way anyone or anything is perceived tends to be reduced to just three descriptive words that may be positive or negative. I call this the Rule of Three."™

"Now wait just a minute," Kyle Otey insisted. "I'm much more complex than just three measly words!"

"Of course you are," the Eagle replied. "It's truly an humbling experience to see your glorious, complex self reduced this way. But, that's how perception works, not just here in Wyoming, but throughout the United States of America, and every other country in the world. Amazing, isn't it, given the long list of powerful influences that tug and pull at us.

"The Rule of Three, you see, is based on human nature. As I mentioned yesterday, when we form our perceptions we tend to take very complex concepts, and reduce them to very simple terms. When the tourist called you mean, scary, and dangerous, she was using The Rule of Three in a negative manner. But there are many positive examples of how it works.

"Take Christianity. The Trinity is a very good example of The Rule of Three. God is described as Father. Son. And Holy Ghost."

"I get it!" Kyle Otey exclaimed!

"The Declaration of Independence sums up Democracy as 'Life. Liberty. And the Pursuit of Happiness.' "

"Exactly! the Eagle agreed. Thomas Jefferson had a very good sense of the Rule of Three when he took the very complex subject of Democracy and reduced it to his famous and stirring words of wisdom."

"Kyle Otey scratched his head, then said, "I guess that if it's good enough for Christianity, and good enough for Democracy, then The Rule of Three may be good enough for you and me, Brandin.

"I don't like it, but I get it."

Rule 3:
The Rule of Three

**How you perceive
yourself and others,
and
how any other person
perceives you,**

**tends to be reduced to
three descriptive words**

**that may be
positive or negative.**

Chapter Eleven
Know Yourself

"Think of it this way, the Eagle said: "We all have our favorite brands that we believe in, trust, and remain loyal to. As I hope I have made clear – each of us has our own Personal Brand.

"If we want others, to believe in, trust, and remain loyal to us, we have to work just as hard to maintain the strength of our Personal Brand – just as Jello and Coke do as brand leaders in the supermarket.

"And by the way, The 7 Rules of Perception work the same way with any brand – whether you are a person or a product.

"Gaining control of
perception begins
within each of us
accepting responsibility
for our own Personal Brand:
developing self-awareness,
a positive self-image,
and a healthy amount
of self-esteem."

"As I've said before, how do you expect to be perceived positively by others if you don't perceive yourself in a positive manner? It's all about attitude. Do you see the glass half full or half empty?

"So let me ask you this, Brandin: when in all of your life experiences did you feel that others were seeing the real you?"

"When I wore down the matador in the bull ring," Brandin replied with no hesitation.

"And, how did you feel at that precise moment?" the Eagle inquired.

"I felt powerful, determined, and successful."

"Are those the three words that sum up how you want to be seen by others?"

"Yes," Brandin answered. "Those are my three words."

"So let's look at how the crowd reacted when you behaved as you wish to be seen; when you showed the real you. The crowd knew what they were seeing, and they were impressed, weren't they? And, by the way, you were not playing to the crowd. You were showing your authentic self, not some made-up figment of your imagination."

"What about Shakespeare?" Kyle Otey countered. "Didn't he say something about the world being a stage and we're all players on it?"

"That's the play, *Hamlet*, and Hamlet is a tragic figure. Not the type of person you should identify with."

Rule 4:
Know Your Three Words

**The three words
that best sum up
who you are
in a positive manner
is your
Personal Brand.**

》》》

Chapter Twelve
Don't Lose Control

"Now that you know about the Rule of Three," the Eagle said, "let's think about the three words that the tourist yelled at you. Remember Brandin, when the tourist called you mean, scary, and dangerous, her three words were her view of reality. I repeat, her view. That doesn't mean that you have to lie down and accept it.

"That's no way to gain confidence and self-respect!" Kyle Otey declared. "Do ya think I'd let hunters bump me off without putting up a fight? My favorite boxer, Jake LaMotta, was called 'The Bull,' not Bambi!"

Brandin didn't feel one bit like Jake LaMotta. In fact he felt pretty meek and ineffectual; not at all comfortable in his own hide.

The Eagle, extended a wing to pat Brandin's shoulder and said, "Don't despair. You have what it takes to control perception – once you learn how to make it work for you.

"You can't just sit around and let others define who you are. As you learned from your experience with the tourist, her perception was full of misinformation which is difficult to change. Particularly if you buy into the idea that you are mean, scary and dangerous – you can't expect to be seen as fearless, strong and brave.

"Step one is to stop playing the victim, for heaven's sake! Take charge and become pro-active. You have the power to change how you are perceived!"

Rule 5:
Don't Lose Control

**If you allow others
to define who you are,
their perceptions may be
full of misinformation
which is difficult to change.**

꒐ ꒐ ꒐

Chapter Thirteen
Branding Yourself

"I've created an exercise that I think you'll find interesting; perhaps even a bit illuminating," the Eagle said to Brandin. "I'm going to leave you alone now - my 7,000 feathers could use a breather - and while I'm gone I want you to take the exercise. It's based on the Rule of Three."

Brandin sat down by a rock, and while Kyle Otey snoozed nearby, he opened to page one.

Ask yourself the questions
on the following two pages.
Please come up with the answers
to each question
in one minute or less.
It is important that you put down
what first comes to mind.

1. Using just three words (or short phrases) describe how you perceive yourself:

_____ _____ _____

2. Using just three words (or short phrases) describe how you think you are perceived by others:

_____ _____ _____

3. Using just three words (or short phrases) describe how you would most like to be perceived by others:

_____ _____ _____

4. Using just three words (or short phrases) describe how you would most NOT like to be perceived by others:

_____ _____ _____

5. If there is a difference between perception and reality (how you answered questions 1 through 4) why does this gap exist ?

_____   _____   _____

6. Name three things that you can do that would help close the gap between perception and reality?

_____   _____   _____

7. Name three things that could PREVENT you from closing the gap between perception and reality?

_____   _____   _____

The Personal Branding Exercise Assessment begins on page 102.
Look for Brandin's answers on page 100.

Chapter Fourteen
The PvP Principle™

After a break for lunch, the Eagle said, "We all have our favorite brands of cars, soaps, and soft drinks. And we remain loyal to the brands we believe in – which is why they are brand leaders. As Muriel Murphy said, 'What you see is what you get.'

"Your Personal Brand works the same way," the Eagle continued. "The goal is to have unity between how you perceive yourself and how others perceive you.

"I call it PvP: Perception *Inside* versus Perception *Outside*. When there is unity between the two, you have *high* PvP. When there is a disconnect between Perception *Inside* and Perception *Outside*, you have *low* PvP."

The Eagle grew silent for a moment, and then pointed a wing towards a steep cliff. "One of my daughters who is extraordinarily beautiful used to spend her afternoons sunning all alone up on that cliff. It pained her that no one seemed to appreciate her intelligence, kindness, and creativity. She saw her beauty as a curse.

"One day, a vulture who was ogling her became so distracted that he ran smack into the head wall of the cliff! My daughter felt so sorry for the poor creature that she came back down to earth.

"Now she's making millions producing nature films for PBS. She's more beautiful than ever, and I hear comments all the time about how brilliant, kind, and creative she is. Her PvP is high as it can be. Just like Oprah's!"

"Wish it were that easy for me," Kyle Otey groused. "My family sees me entirely differently than the outside world does – just like Michael Corlione in *The Godfather*. Talk about a disconnect between home and the office. Makes me have warm feelings for Martha Stewart!' "

"Your problem, Kyle, is that you see such a disconnect as the norm, when it really is not," the Eagle cautioned. The great brands are very consistent and persistent in the way they are perceived. And their manufacturers make darn certain that it stays that way. Jell-O IS Jell-O. And Kleenex IS Kleenex. They know that the perceived value of their brand name is priceless because customers remain loyal to a brand they know and trust.

"The same is true for people. Strong Personal Brands remain in control of perception. They have a a clear sense of who and what they are about. They are consistent and persistent in expressing who and what they are about. And they do not let events overwhelm their resolve.

"It's really healthier to be consistent – like John Wayne. In the political world they call it 'sticking to message.' That's why George Bush is President and Al Gore is not. Al kept changing his three words every debate."

"Is there any chance I can stick to message?" Brandin asked.

"More than a chance, Brandin. I have a feeling that you're going to hit the bulls-eye!"

Rule 6:
The PvP™ Principle

**There should be
unity between
how you perceive yourself,
and
how others perceive you.**

🔊 🔊 🔊

Chapter 15
Branding Someone You Know

"When Kyle Otey woke up from his aftenroon siesta, Brandin had finished his Personal Branding Exercise and the Eagle had just reappeared. "Now, It's your turn."

"You talkin' to me? Kyle Otey said with his best Robert DeNiro swagger.

"You're the one, the Eagle replied. "I want you and Brandin to use the Rule of Three to describe each other. This is a good way to check whether there is unity between how you perceive yourself, and how others perceive you - Perception *Inside* versus Perception *Outside*.

"I don't know if I'm gonna like this, Kyle Otey muttered. But, as Mama Otey says, "If you can't take the heat get out of the den."

Exercise #2
Branding Someone You Know

As you did with Exercise #1, please come up with the answers to the following questions in one minute or less. It is important that you put down what first comes to mind.

1. Using just three words (or short phrases) describe how you think (*person you select*) perceives himself or herself:

_____ _____ _____

2. Using just three words (or short phrases) describe how you think (*person you select*) thinks he or she is perceived by others:

_____ _____ _____

3. Using just three words (or short phrases) describe how you think (*person you select*) would most LIKE to be perceived by others:

_____ _____ _____

4. Using just three words (or short phrases) describe how you think (*person you select*) would most NOT LIKE to be perceived by others:

_____ _____ _____

5. If there is a difference between Perception *Inside* and Perception *Outside* (how you answered questions 1 through 4) why does this gap exist ?

_____ _____ _____

6. Name three things that you think (person you select) can do that would help *close the gap* between perception and reality?

_____ _____ _____

7. Name three things that could PREVENT (*person you select*) from closing the gap

_____ _____ _____

Look for the assessment on page 108.
Brandin's answers to this exercise are on page 106.

When the Eagle showed Kyle Otey how Brandin had described him in the exercise, the hairs stuck up straight on his back and he blurted out, "Now wait just a minute. That's what you think of me? Well, Kyle Otey's gonna prove you wrong!"

The Eagle calmed Kyle Otey down by reassuring him that the exercise has many positive benefits. "I did it with my daughter and it led to the best talk we've had in years!"

"Just remember that the object of the lesson is to help you understand that we don't always see ourselves as others do."

ꙮ ꙮ ꙮ

Chapter Sixteen
Practice Makes Perfect

"So tell me this, Brandin," The Eagle asked: "Do you think that you have the inner fortitude and the resolve to gain control of perception? To express who and what you truly are in a consistent and persistent manner?

"I ask you this question because I have an idea that I want to pursue. But, before I waste my time, you must make a commitment: Promise me that you will practice every day – in every way that you can imagine – how to project to the world that you are strong, determined, and successful. The way you were in the bull ring.

"I'll be giving you my Eagle eye. And when I'm convinced that you understand The 7 Rules of Perception, and that you've learned how to apply them to gain control of perception, I'll return."

Rule 7:
Be Consistent

**Express the three words
that best describe who you
are
(your Personal Brand)
with confidence
and
consistency.**

From that day forwards, Brandin faithfully practiced how to project his true self to the world. From the time he got up in the morning, to the moment he drifted off to sleep, he tried different ways of expressing power, determination, and success.

One day, he came upon a rattlesnake poised to strike. But instead of fleeing in terror, Brandin stood his ground, fought his fear, pawed the ground, and was pleasantly surprised – and relieved – when the snake scurried away.

"O.K., so you were lucky today," Kyle Otey muttered. "But as my dear mother was known to say, 'One snake a new perception does not make.'"

Brandin ignored Kyle Otey, best as he could, and stuck to his course.

**Brandin's
inner voice
(and strengths)
were coming
to life.**

ꙿ ꙿ ꙿ

Chapter Seventeen
Picture This!

Several months later, in the late afternoon, just as the light was turning pale gold against the mountaintops, mounds of dust trailing the wheels of a fast moving truck appeared over the horizon. The Eagle was perched on its tailgate.

The truck ground to a stop, and out stepped a tall, handsome man with white hair peaking from beneath a broad brimmed cowboy hat. Without any hesitation, he strode up to Brandin, and in a low, commanding voice said, "If what the Eagle tells me about you is true, then I think we have the makings of a deal that will be mutually beneficial."

Realizing his opportunity, and remembering his promise to the Eagle, Brandin felt a sudden surge of confidence. He stood tall as he could, his broad chest swelling with pride.

The man put his hands on his hips, and fixed his eyes on Brandin who, in turn, never for a second took his eyes off the rich rancher.

The Eagle and Kyle Otey watched the two size one another up for what seemed like an eternity. And then, the rancher said to the Eagle, "You're right. This bull is just what we've been looking for. Be at the airport at seven in the morning, Brandin. You and I are gonna take a little trip."

And so, bright and early the next day, Brandin traveled in the luxury of the rancher's private jet to the biggest airport he had ever seen, its horizon dominated by huge skyscrapers. Waiting for him was a fancy vehicle with the words, "Bull Mobile" emblazoned on its side in glittering gold letters.

Brandin felt totally ridiculous standing alone in the bright green, flatbed truck as it moved towards the center of the big city.

The truck turned a corner, and Brandin froze. Stretching ahead was an extremely narrow street paved with cobblestones. Crowds of people were hanging out of windows screaming and yelling, and packed six-deep along the sidewalks straining for a look at the Bull Mobile.

It all seemed too familiar.

Suddenly, the sky filled with white flecks that looked like a blizzard of snow even though it was a warm, summer day. Brandin was so confused that he felt close to fainting, but just in the nick of time, the rancher – now dressed in a finely tailored pin-stripe suit – jumped up onto the Bull Mobile and shouted, "Well Brandin, how do you like all this adulation? This Wall Street ticker tape parade is bigger than the ones for Lindbergh, John Glenn – even the New York Yankees. "Look how the people love you! The way they're cheering for you!

"Cheering for me? But why?" Brandin asked, totally puzzled.

"Because you're the new symbol of power, determination and success! The Eagle told me your story, and when I heard about your courage in the bull ring, I had a hunch that you're just the inspiration Wall Street needs – given all the problems the stock market's been having of late.

"Starting today, Brandin, you're the new symbol of the Bull Market, and believe me, EVERYONE loves a Bull Market. From now on, when people see you, they'll feel a reassuring sense of strength and security – and those are mighty good feelings to have in today's uncertain world."

And so dear readers you'll be happy to know that from that day forwards the power, determination, and success that Brandin so wished was his perception became his reality.

Back to the ranch in the mountains in Wyoming he journeyed to spend the rest of his days in a brand new bull pen complete with a special wing built especially for his sisters, and his mother, Molly.

Brandin lived a happy and contented life, accepted as he had never been accepted before. A steady stream of visitors flocked to the ranch eager to have their picture taken with the brave bull, and to return home with a bottle of Kyle Otey's Wicked Wyoming Chicken Marinade.

And not a single person
ran away when Brandin
came up to say hi.

))))))

THE END

The Seven Rules of Perception™

Exercise Assessments

Questions to Ask Yourself

The 7 Rules of Perception

1. Perception is Reality

How you perceive yourself
(or any other person) is your reality.
How any other person perceives you
(whether fair or not) is his or her reality.

2. Powerful Influences

Many factors influence how you form your
perceptions about yourself and others, and
how others form their perceptions about you.

3. The Rule of Three

How you perceive yourself and others,
and how any other person perceives you,
tends to be reduced to three descriptive
words that may be positive or negative.

4. Know Your Three Words

The three words that best sum up
who you are in a positive manner
is your Personal Brand.

5. Don't Lose Control

If you allow others to define who you are, their
perceptions may be full of misinformation
which is very difficult to change.

6. The PvP™ Principle

There should be unity between how you
perceive yourself and how others perceive you.

7. Be Consistent

Express the three words that best describe
who you are with confidence and consistency.

⦿))) ⦿))) ⦿))

Brandin's Answers to the
Personal Branding Exercise

1. Using just three words (or short phrases) describe how you perceive yourself:

   Loyal   Loving   Unappreciated

2. Using just three words (or short phrases) describe how you think you are perceived by others:

   Strong   Scary   Dangerous

3. Using just three words (or short phrases) describe how you would most like to be perceived by others:

   Powerful   Determined   Successful

4. Using just three words (or short phrases) describe how you would most NOT like to be perceived by others:

_____Mean_____   _____Scary_____   _____dangerous_____

5. If there is a difference between perception and reality (how you answered questions 1 through 4) why does this gap exist ?

_____appearance_____   _____ignorance_____   _____bull fights_____

6. Name three things that you can do that would help close the gap between perception and reality?

_____know myself_____   _____express myself_____   _____be confident_____

7. Name three things that could PREVENT you from closing the gap between perception and reality?

_____fearful_____   _____lack of ambition_____   _____inconsistent_____

⟫ ⟫ ⟫

Personal Branding
Exercise Assessment

You've done it! Your own, private analysis of how you are perceived by others – and how you perceive yourself. And it only took about ten minutes! Each of us, deep down, has a pretty good handle on our own PvP (Perception *Inside* versus Perception *Outside*).

The Personal Branding Exercise is designed to be brief and to-the-point. It's easier to compare concepts this way. If you had trouble answering questions with just one word, that's ok. Go back and try the exercise again using a short phrase.

For instance, you might say, "lack of sensitivity" instead of "insensitive." Or how about "afraid of failing" instead of "insecure." Just write that thought down best as you can.

a. Compare the three words you chose in **Question #1** to the three words you chose in **Question #2** to determine your PvP, how close Perception Inside is to Perception Outside. How you view yourself in Question #1 should be close to your answers in Question #2. If your answers are close together, you have high PvP, and a strong Personal Brand identity. If your answers are far apart, you have low PvP, and a weak Personal Brand identity.

b. Compare the words that you chose in **Questions #2 and #3.** Again, how you think others perceive you and how you would like to be perceived should be as close together as possible. Are your answers close or far apart? The closer they are the HIGHER your PvP, and the STRONGER your Personal Brand identity. The further apart your answers are, the LOWER your PvP, and the WEAKER your Personal Brand.

d. Question #5 is revealing. You are providing

yourself with important information about what you need to do to change, and to bring Perception Inside closer to Perception Outside. The third word you chose is often quite telling – perhaps the most difficult word for you to admit to, and acknowledge.

e. Question #6 is the beginning of self-actualization – of being perceived as you truly are. These three words form the foundation of your action plan for change. They describe what you believe you can realistically do to bring Perception Inside closer to Perception Outside.

f. Question #7 is another aspect of self-actualization. It shows what you are afraid of – what you think may prevent you from becoming the person you want to be perceived as. These three words are hard to accept, but must be overcome if you want to change how you are perceived.

PLEASE NOTE: The Personal Branding Exercise is not meant to take the place of expert counselors and therapists if that is what you need.

The Exercise is simply a useful tool to assess Perception Inside versus Perception Outside, and to gain insight about what you can do to take corrective action if you do not like how you are perceived.

Discuss the Exercise with parents and friends; meet with a counselor, coach or therapist. And use the Personal Branding Exercise to help guide your discussions. The point is: you have identified your PvP issues.

Now get on with it!

Brandin's Explanation
of Kyle Otey
Branding Someone
You Know

1. Using just three words (or short phrases) describe how you think (*person you select*) perceives himself or herself:

<u>cocky</u>   <u>cynical</u>   <u>insecure</u>

2. Using just three words (or short phrases) describe how you think (*person you select*) thinks he or she is perceived by others:

<u>sly</u>   <u>sneaky</u>   <u>not to be trusted</u>

3. Using just three words (or short phrases) describe how you think (*person you select*) would most LIKE to be perceived by others:

<u>brilliant</u>   <u>creative</u>   <u>entrepreneur</u>

4. Using just three words (or short phrases) describe how you think (*person you select*) would most NOT LIKE to be perceived by others:

<u>stupid</u>   <u>lazy</u>   <u>loser</u>

5. If there is a difference between Perception *Inside* and Perception *Outside* (how you answered questions 1 through 4) why does this gap exist ?

<u>stereotyping</u>   <u>ignorance</u>   <u>myths</u>

6. Name three things that you think (person you select) can do that would help *close the gap* between perception and reality?

<u>speak out</u>   <u>show loving side</u>   <u>listen better</u>

7. Name three things that could PREVENT (*person you select*) from closing the gap between perception and reality?

<u>laziness</u>   <u>insecurity</u>   <u>poverty</u>

》》》

Branding Someone
You Know
Exercise Assessment

a. Compare the three words you chose in
Question #1 to the three words you chose in
Question #2 to determine how close Perception
Inside is to Perception *Outside*. How you view
the person you described in Question #1 should
be close to your answers in Question #2. If they
are, the person you selected has HIGH PvP, and
a STRONG Personal Brand identity. If your
answers are far apart, the person you selected has
LOW PvP, and a weak Personal Brand identity.

b. Compare the words that you chose in
Questions #2 and #3. How you perceive person
you selected, and how you think he or she would

like to be perceived, should be as close together as possible. Are your answers close or far apart? The closer they are the HIGHER the PvP, and the STRONGER the Personal Brand identity of the person you selected.. The further apart your answers are, the LOWER the PvP, and the WEAKER the person's Personal Brand Identity.

d. Question #5 is revealing. You are describing what the person you selected needs to do to change, and to bring Perception Inside closer to Perception Outside. The third word you chose is often quite telling - perhaps the most difficult word to admit to.

e. Question #6 describes what you believe the person you selected can *realistically* do to bring Perception Inside closer to Perception Outside - to be seen as he or she truly is.
f. Question #7 is another aspect of self-

actualization. It shows what you think the person you chose is afraid of – what you think may *prevent* he or she from becoming the person you think he or she would like to be perceived as. These three words but *must* be overcome if meaningful change is to take place.

)))))))

Questions to Ask Yourself

1. Which character in this book do you most identify with? _____
Why? _____
_____
_____

2. Which character do you least identify with?
_____
Why? _____
_____
_____

3. Who reminds you of Brandin?
_____
_____
_____

4. Who reminds you of Kyle Otey?

_____

_____

_____

5. Who reminds you of the Eagle?

_____

_____

_____

6. What did you learn about yourself by doing the Personal Branding Exercise?

_____

_____

_____

_____

7. What was Brandin afraid of that prevented him from revealing his true self?

_____

_____

_____

_____

8. What happened to Brandin in the bull ring? And how did it change him?

_____

_____

_____

_____

9. What can you do that would help others see you as you truly are?

_____

_____

_____

_____

10. How does Brandin The Bull deal with profiling and stereotyping?

_____

_____

_____

_____

11. Have you ever experienced profiling or stereotyping in your personal life? _____
At work? _____
In your community? _____

How did it express itself?

_____

_____

_____

How did you feel?

_____

_____

_____

What did you do about it?

_____

_____

_____

Services

Services

Educate! Inspire! Motivate!
• Inspirational books   • Consulting
• Training programs   • Merchandising
• Speaking Engagements

Topics include:

Brand Leadership
    Creating a Brand
    Maintaining a Brand
    Saving a Brand

Personal Success - How the 7 Rules of Perception
    can change your life

Customer Service - To the customer,
    "I AM" the brand. Starring Kyle Otey,
    Chicken Billionaire.

Corporate Change - Why we resist it.

Office Politics - Wanda Pesky and the
    Weasel, and other horror stories

Leadership - What you see is what you get.

Diversity - Combatting profiling and stereotyping.

Team Building - Using the Personal Branding
    Exercise to build self-awareness
    and communication.

Targeted programs for:

Fortune 500 companies
Small Businesses
Institutions and
Organizations
Health Care

Retail stores
Restaurants
Hotels/Motels
Real Estate
Politics

Multiple Applications:

Sales and Marketing
Building A New Brand
Maintaining Brand Leadership
Repairing a Brand Gone Bad
Customer Service Training
Sales Training

Management
Leadership Development
Organizational Development
Team Building
Corporate Change
Increasing Productivity

Human Resources
Recruitment
Employee Retention
Diversity Training
Office Politics

Memorable Merchandising

**Combine your logo with the PERCEPTION RULES!
logo, characters and themes applied to:**

T-shirts	Hats
Mugs	Totes
Post-It Notes	Calendars
Posters	Pens
Golf balls	Reminder Cards
Bookmarks	Mouse Pads
Screen Savers	

Also available:
Animated videos;
Audio CD's and tapes.

Flexibility and Value:
• Turn-key as well as full
service options.
• All books available in hard and
soft cover; short books,
and booklets

Universal Appeal:
Since perception is based on human nature
PERCEPTION RULES! has worldwide applications.

Our books feature animal characters and stories
that cross over cultrual & ethnic boundaries.

Licensing Opportunities

Ask about our lucrative domestic and global licensing
opportunities to represent the Bulls Eye Branding
metod including PERCEPTION RULES! books,
training and consulting programs, and merchandising.

The Publisher of PERCEPTION RULES!
series of self-help business books is

Ordering

The PERCEPTION RULES!
business library includes:

PERCEPTION RULES!
Personal Success
The Story of Brandin, the Misunderstood Bull

PERCEPTION RULES!
Brand Leadership
The Wisdom of Kyle Otey, Chicken Billionaire

PERCEPTION RULES!
Fear of Change
The Transformation of Melvin

PERCEPTION RULES!
Office Politics
The Story of Wanda Pesky and The Weasel

PERCEPTION RULES!
Customer Satisfaction
You ARE the Brand!
More Wisdom from Kyle Otey, Chicken Billionaire.

Acknowledgements

In theory, Brandin the Bull took a lifetime to write; in actuality, 2 and a half years. Distilling decades of life experience into the story of a misunderstood bull does not come easy.

Helping me along the way were friends who cojoled me, prodded me, encouraged me, critiqued me, and most important of all – listened to me, believed in me, and took me into their homes when I needed a break from the routine. Thank you so, my dear friends. You're all on the jet!

My children, Ned and Kate Harris, are the joy of my life, and nothing will make me happier than their seeing my hard work succeed. They – like so many others – adored my mother who is the voice of the Eagle, and she adored them.

Some people were especially helpful as wise eyes and helpful guides in the editing and design process: Thank you Lyndsay, Cynthia and Richard, Jill, Sandy, Nancy, Sebby, Karen, Leslie, Gary, William, Bev and Jack, Jimmy, Stanley, Marion, Joyce, Katherine, Bobbie and Roland, Peter, Peg, and Mary.

Even those who were not with me helped me understand and appreciate that, like it or not, PERCEPTION RULES!

V Harris
September, 2003

Notes

Notes

Notes

Notes